CASE
TRACTORS

Andrew Morland & Nick Baldwin

Motorbooks International
Publishers & Wholesalers ®

First published in 1996 by Motorbooks International Publishers & Wholesalers, 729 Prospect Avenue, PO Box 1, Osceola, WI 54020-0001 USA

The information in this book is true and complete to the best of our knowledge. All recommendations are made without any guarantee on the part of the author or Publisher, who also disclaim any liability incurred in connection with the use of this data or specific details

We recognize that some words, model names and designations, for example, mentioned herein are the property of the trademark holder. We use them for identification purposes only. This is not an official publication

Motorbooks International books are also available at discounts in bulk quantity for industrial or sales-promotional use. For details write to Special Sales Manager at the Publisher's address

Library of Congress Cataloging-in-Publication Data Available

ISBN 0-7603-0093-3

On the front cover: A Case Model S built in 1944. The S Series was produced between 1941 and 1954 and became the third-best-selling gasoline Case tractor. This fine example is owned by J. R. Gyger.

On the frontispiece: In 1939, the R Series received Flambeau Red paint and streamlined styling. The focal point of the new design was this cast-iron sunburst radiator grille.

On the title page: The 10-20 three-wheeled tractor was priced at under $900. Between 1915 and 1918, Case built 6,679 of these tractors. Despite the unconventional appearance, the modern four-cylinder, overhead valve lightweight engine helped sell this tractor.

On the back cover: The Model 25-45 of 1925. In the November 1924 Nebraska tests, the 25-45 produced, at 850rpm, 45.18hp at the belt and 32.96hp at the drawbar. This powerful tractor is owned by Ed Lammers.

Printed in Hong Kong

CONTENTS

ACKNOWLEDGMENTS

Thank you to all the enthusiastic owners of Case tractors in America whose help and co-operation made this book possible.

A very special thank you to the following for not only helping with the photography of their Case tractors, but also for their very generous hospitality during my visits.

Albert and Evelyn Remme
Russell, Edith, Ried, and Linda Church
Ed Lammers
Ed and Carla Schutch
John Davis
Norm Seviek
the Gyger family

Thanks also to the Ford Motor Co. for the use of their Ranger Splash pickup for my photographic travels.

There are two enthusiastic Case clubs in the U.S.A., both with quarterly magazines and friendly knowledgeable Case experts. Anyone interested in becoming a member can contact the following addresses:

J. I. Case Collectors Association, Inc.,
in care of Crooked Hollow
Farm Publishing,
4004 Coal Valley Road,
Vinton, Ohio 45686-9741;
and
J. I. Case Heritage Foundation,
Box 5128
Bella Vista, Arkansas
72714-0128.

INTRODUCTION

Jerome Increase Case, born in 1819, started a threshing machine manufacturing business in 1842. He located his workshop in Rochester, Wisconsin, but an argument over water rights led him to move to nearby Racine in 1844. Here, he became the biggest employer for miles around and built all types of threshing machines. A few years later, Case took as its emblem the Civil War bald eagle mascot Old Abe (named after President Lincoln), which continued to grace Case machinery for the next 105 years. It was a great way to build name recognition—and by 1923, Case had manufactured 100,000 threshing machines.

It soon became obvious that steam was a more satisfactory source of static power than horses harnessed in "horse engines," and in 1869 Case built the first of a long line of some 36,000 steam engines. One drawback of the steam engine was that during threshing the combination of fire, dust, and chaff could cause the wooden threshing machine to catch fire. Case got around this in 1904 by developing an all-steel threshing machine.

1876 saw J. I. Case create an additional business at Racine under the name of Case, Whiting & Company to build plows. It quickly became known as the J. I. Case Plow Works. Because it had no corporate connection with J. I. Case & Company (which became the J. I. Case Threshing Machine Company in 1880), both firms ultimately became rivals when they developed similar products. Among these, in time, were tractors. The first step on this route for the J. I. Case Threshing Machine Company came in 1876, when it began to develop steam traction engines. These became the most widely sold in the world in the early years of the twentieth century and carried on right through to 1924, when internal combustion began to prove its superiority.

These traction engines did vast amounts of work. For example, a 25-75hp unit costing $1,800 in 1910 was used in Canada for grading roads, pulling tree stumps, and breaking prairie soil. It helped to shift grain stores and buildings and threshed more than one million bushels of grain, wearing out two separators in the process.

An even bigger 32-110hp traction engine was sold in 1912 to George Langley, who was to become a prominent Canadian government minister. Hauling a twelve-bottom plow with extra-wide driving wheels for maximum grip and minimum compaction, it could turn thirty-five to forty acres in a 16hr day.

The great pioneer Jerome Increase Case died in 1891 and was replaced at the helm of the company he had founded by his brother-in-law, Stephen Bull, who directed Case's first experiments with an internal combustion engine tractor the following year. The so-called Case-Paterson was built on traction engine lines but with a two-cylinder four-stroke spark-ignition engine, and single forward and reverse gears. Problems with carburetion and ignition on the engine, which was designed by William Paterson, are given as the reason that this and some succeeding prototype tractors got no further. However, one can imagine that Case's commitment to steam must have been at the heart of the decision to abandon what was one of the world's earliest recognizable tractors.

The J. I. Case Threshing Machine Co. did not return to the internal combustion engine market until 1911. Stephen's son Frank had taken up the reigns at J. I. Case. In the meantime, another relative of J. I. Case had taken command up the road at the Plow Works. He was H. M. Wallis, who also happened to own the Wallis Tractor Co. of Cleveland, Ohio, where, in 1902, the Bear gas tractor was created. This was a monstrous affair of tricycle layout with a wide roller-type front wheel, forward-mounted engine, and large-traction engine rear wheels, between which the operator stood.

A series of 20 and 40hp models followed before the most famous Wallis of all took to the fields in 1913. By then the Wallis Tractor Co. had begun to consolidate with the J. I. Case Plow Works and had moved to Racine.

The revolutionary Wallis Cub that followed was of unit construction with all-mechanical components, including a four-cylinder 13–25hp engine, mounted on a roller frame made from boiler plate. This ingenious machine was the work of company engineers Clarence Eason and Robert Hendrickson and in 1919 began featuring a fully enclosed drive with a four-wheel layout, as opposed to a three-wheel layout.

Meanwhile, the Threshing Machine Co. had been busy gaining gasoline engine experience. In 1910, it acquired the Pierce Engine Co. in Racine, which had experimented with automobiles as early as 1894 and built them in series from early in the twentieth century. This gave Case an entry into the motor vehicle market, which in 1910 was put to good purpose when it introduced its own Case cars. These were soon followed by the first of a major series of gas tractors, a name given to many such gasoline-powered machines of the early years.

CHAPTER ONE

1911 - 1930

O ne might have expected a firm making cars to have made a relatively lightweight tractor on the lines of the Wallis. However, with its new 30-60hp of 1911, Case remained true to the giant traction engine concept. This two-cylinder twelve-ton giant had a flywheel weighing 1000lb. The engine, and indeed the whole machine, was built for Case by the makers of the Twin City tractor. This was the Minneapolis Steel & Machinery Co. which, confusingly, like the two Case companies, had a rival concern of similar name (the Minneapolis Threshing Machine Co.), whose Minneapolis-Moline tractors lasted until their takeover by White in 1963. Around 500 Case 30-60 tractors were sold into 1916, the first of which won a Gold Medal in the 1911 Winnipeg Plowing Contest.

In 1912, the 30-60 was joined by a 20-40 with a Davis twin-cylinder engine, which again won Gold at Winnipeg. This important tractor accounted for almost 4,300 sales before its demise in 1920—an impressive total until one appreciates that the U. S. tractor industry as a whole turned out more

The 80hp Case traction engine has an 11x11in single-cylinder engine. It is seen here at the Western Minnesota Steam Threshers Reunion at Rollag, Minnesota.

The 110hp Case traction engine has a 12x12in single-cylinder engine. Built in 1913, these 18-ton traction engines were used for plowing with ten- or twelve-bottom plows on the prairie wheat fields. Photographed at Rollag, Minnesota, on Labor Day. Owned by Jim Briden and Norman Pross of North Dakota.

RIGHT
A Case 65hp, single-cylinder traction engine built in 1916. Photographed at the North Central Steam and Gas Engine Club Show at Edgar, Wisconsin. Owned by Gary Schacht.

The Case trademark transfer on the water tank of a 1913 80hp traction engine shows the J. I. Case Threshing Machine factory on the river at Racine, Wisconsin.

than 200,000 machines in 1920, a substantial increase from the 15,000 produced in 1914. The 20-40 looked less like a steam traction engine as it neared the end of production, thanks in part to a gilled tube radiator with cast-iron header tank and sides instead of the traditional "water tower" resembling a steam funnel. It also had a full-length canopy to protect the operator and two horizontally opposed cylinders lying longitudinally in the frame.

Nineteen-thirteen marked the construction of a dedicated tractor plant at Racine known as the Clausen Works which was named after Leon Clausen, who became President in 1924. In 1924, the factory employed 3,000, and steam engines and automobiles were axed. Looking more like an enclosed tractor of the 1920s was the 12-25, current for five years from 1913. Its conventional radiator and hood, however, belied the fact that it was still built on a channel steel frame and had a two-cylinder engine, with its crankshaft in line with its gear-driven rear wheels. More than 3,300 of this

more compact model were sold, a figure which itself was half that of the new 10-20 of 1915 onwards. This three-wheeler at last had an overhead valve automotive-type four-cylinder engine, which lay across the frame and drove a single roller-like wheel in line astern from the single-steered front wheel. A land wheel stabilized this first lightweight Case, from which evolved the famous cross-motor Cases of 1916–1928. This family was born with the 9-18, which after a brief spell with a channel frame became in 1918 the 9-18B with cast-iron frame. Fordson had pioneered this ingenious way of lightening and cheapening tractor construction after studying the boiler plate Wallis and others.

Meanwhile, what of the Wallis, which in cultivator form in 1919 even dared to wear the name J. I. Case, though not Old Abe, on its radiator?

The original tricycle-type Wallis was replaced in 1919 with the four-wheeled Model K, which for a time was sold in Canada by Fairbanks Morse. Agricultural machinery maker Massey-Harris then assumed Canadian distribution and in 1928 purchased the J. I. Case Plow Works. This at last put an end to customers' confusion about the two Case factories. Massey-Harris then sold its rights in the J. I. Case name to the J. I. Case Threshing Machine Co. to recover much of the original purchase price and end the confusion once and for all. The Plow Co. then changed its name to the Massey-Harris Company of Racine, and under this title continued to make Wallis tractors for a while before introducing modernized versions under its own name.

Ed Schuth of Wabasha, Minnesota, at the controls of his 10-20 Case, built in 1918. The 5,000lb tractor with four-cylinder engine produced 20 belt hp at 900rpm and over 10hp at the drawbar using kerosene. This three-bottom plow tractor has a one speed transmission.

Incidentally, Massey-Harris' first tractors in the teens had not been its own designs but those of Bull and then Parrett.

Back at the Threshing Machine Co., a revised 9-18B became the 10-18, which with its crossmotor predecessors finally put Case in the big time with around 15,000 sales. In 1919, Case bought the Grand Detour Plow Co. of Grand Detour, Illinois, to expand its line of farm machinery. Combine harvesters became big business in 1923, though it was to be another thirty years before threshing machines were omitted from the Case range.

Perhaps anticipating this, the business simplified its name in 1928 to the J. I. Case Company and went on another shopping spree, this time acquiring agricultural machinery and tractor maker Emerson-Brantingham of Rockford, Illinois. The roots of this business lay in a reaping machine created around the time that J. I. Case was starting work in Racine. Emerson-Brantingham itself acquired many other tractor designs over the years and, as well as the Reeves and Big 4, made its own E-B types, with an unusually low hood line, right up to its takeover by Case.

The 10-20 Case with single front wheel and arrow to show the steering direction. The operator sitting at the rear would have no view of the front wheel.

The crossmotor Case was winning friends all over the world. Its advantages included a straight-forward layout with the engine weight close to the driven wheels and a short wheelbase for maneuverability. Like most of its contemporaries, it started on gasoline and then, when warm enough, could be switched to cheaper kerosene. Several sizes of the crossmotor were available: the 15-27, 18-32, 22-40, 25-45, and 40-72. These horsepower classifications show horsepower exerted at the drawbar in the first figure and belt pulley horsepower in the second. These were conservative figures under the Case system, as confirmed by a 40-72 tested at Nebraska which actually recorded a maximum of 49.8 and 91.4hp under working conditions. A 15-27 in similar circumstances recorded 18.8 and 31.2hp.

A Case won the Gold Medal in the up to 24hp category at the 1920 Lincoln Tractor Trials in England. In second place was a Cletrac crawler. By then, Case had established agencies in Britain, Brazil, France, and Uruguay, as well as a short-lived one in Russia.

Plainly, there was greatest demand for the smallest and cheapest of the crossmotor models, which were far more expensive than the new Fordsons. In the British market for example, the 25.6hp Fordson fell from £280 in 1920 to £120 in 1922, whereas the 10-18 and 15-27 Case cost £235 and £375 in the latter year. The importer Associated Manufacturers Co. (London) Ltd., well known for its Amanco farm engines, made the point in 1926 that, *"Only the best is good enough; price doesn't count. Case 12-20hp models have now been running over three years without overhaul or*

A 12-20 Case built in 1927 with four-cylinder, overhead-valve crossmotor engine rated at 20 belt hp and 12 drawbar hp. Owner Russell Church is at the controls on his dairy farm near Minnesota City, Minnesota.

RIGHT
The Case 15-27 crossmotor of 1920 showing the twin disc clutch fitted inside the belt pulley. Note there is easy access to the Berling magneto. The bottom half of the engine sits in the rigid cast-iron frame of the tractor.

The 15-27 Case tractor built in 1920 produced more power at the Nebraska tests that year than Case claimed. The maximum belt horsepower was 31.23, and the drawbar horsepower was 18.80 at 900rpm on kerosene. Owner John Davis of Maplewood, Ohio.

A Case 25-45 crossmotor built in 1925 with a 1941 Case Model VC row crop inside the barn. Owner Ed Lammers of Butterfield, Minnesota.

replacement. They must of course wear out some day, but no one can say yet where they will give out first. This is real tractor consistency, and when is added 25% to 50% more work on less fuel and oil you will know why farmers will have only Case tractors in areas where they are known."

The 12-20, 18-32, and 25-45 were revised as A, K, and T models in 1928, by which time the crossmotor models had notched up almost 50,000 sales. Not surprisingly, the largest 40-72 was by far the rarest, with fewer than fifty machines at work, and these mostly on the largest prairie farms or else towing graders and similar equipment on road and dam construction projects.

Mention has already been made of the ease of maneuvering these relatively short-wheelbase models. The 12-20 had an exemplary turning radius of 12ft. Because of the engine position, the belt pulley was able to run directly off the crankshaft, thus minimizing power loss through gearing. The tractor had two forward gears giving 2.2 and 3mph at its engine's normal maximum 1050rpm. The monobloc four-cylinder engine had a one-piece detachable head and overhead valves, an important provision (for the first time on a

The 25-45 Case tractor #52961 built in 1925. The paint on this crossmotor is a shade too dark. It should be LC Gray, the dark shade of gray used from mid-1923 up to 1929. The 25-45 was produced from 1925 to 1928 with only 980 built.

Case) being replaceable cylinder liners. Another unusual feature of the time was a thermostat to control the flow of coolant water. Air for the combustion process went through a water washer, and a mixture of pressure and splash oiling took care of lubrication, the governors receiving oil only when the pressure relief valve opened. Considerable attention was paid to keeping the induction side of the engine heated to optimum temperature by the exhaust for minimum consumption of fuel. All in all, the 12-20 and its

RIGHT
The Case 10-18 built in 1919 was sold as a two-bottom plow tractor with a two-speed transmission. The four-cylinder, overhead-valve crossmotor engine gave a maximum belt horsepower of 23-24 and a maximum drawbar horsepower of 12-14. John Davis of Maplewood, Ohio, is the owner.

sisters were extremely well-thought out machines which endeared themselves to their owners and operators.

As the 1920s progressed, however, it became obvious that Case's layout,

20

The 9-18 was Case's first crossmotor tractor. The engine was mounted on a steel frame.

Crossmotor tractors after 1918 had their engines placed on a one-piece cast-iron frame.

while practical, had not been adopted by most other tractor makers and certainly not by the new breed of general-purpose tractors offered by Ford, Allis-Chalmers, International Harvester, and others. Three speeds became a necessity, and rather than convert farmers to the cross-motor concept, it seemed more sensible for Case to fall in line with the almost-universal trend to have engines mounted conventionally "north-south."

No doubt the acquisition of the Emerson-Brantingham line gave Case the

opportunity to change direction, even though it had been experimenting with a replacement range since the mid-1920s. The E-B was conventional in many ways, but its pinion and ring gear drive in the wheels was vulnerable to damage from grit. Having discontinued the Emerson-Brantinghams, Case had already decided to go for final drive by enclosed roller chain. This might at first be interpreted as a retrograde step, but Case pointed out several advantages, including spreading the torque over more teeth than was possible with gears and minimum power loss through friction.

The new tractors arrived in 1929, commencing with the L Model, a 26-40hp machine with three forward gears and other up-to-date refinements.

RIGHT
The 9-18 Case has the modern overhead-valve, four-cylinder 18 belt hp crossmotor. The engine has a bore and stroke of 3-7/8x5in. It is fitted with a Kingston carburetor and Kingston high tension magneto with impulse starter. The hand clutch is an expanding shoe type.

A 9-18 Case tractor built in 1916, the first year of production. It is a very rare tractor as only twenty-two were built the first year. However, in 1917 and 1918, production nearly hit 5,800 before the 10-18 Case took its sales. This example is owned by Russell Church of Minnesota City, Minnesota.

LEFT

Case Model X Roadster of 1924. The radiator wears the Case trademark showing the famous mascot "Old Abe" of the Eighth Wisconsin regiment. In 1910 Case took over the Pierce Engine Co. car production in Racine, near their own factory on the river. However, despite Case's marketing ability and money, the car company never made a profit, and it closed in 1927. The cars were too expensive, and there were too many quality car manufacturers in the USA at this time.

Case Model X Roadster built in 1924 by J. I. Case, developed from the Pierce-Racine car designed by A. J. Pierce back in 1910. The Model X was the cheapest and smallest model; it had a 3958cc engine. The Model U had a 4957cc six-cylinder Continental engine, and the Y had a 5328cc engine. This car is owned by Stan Sill of Rockford, Ohio.

Case CC built in 1930, a very popular two- or three-bottom plow tractor, with 4,223 built that year. The four-cylinder, overhead-valve engine produces 27 belt hp and 17 drawbar hp at 1100rpm. This CC is owned by Ed Lammers.

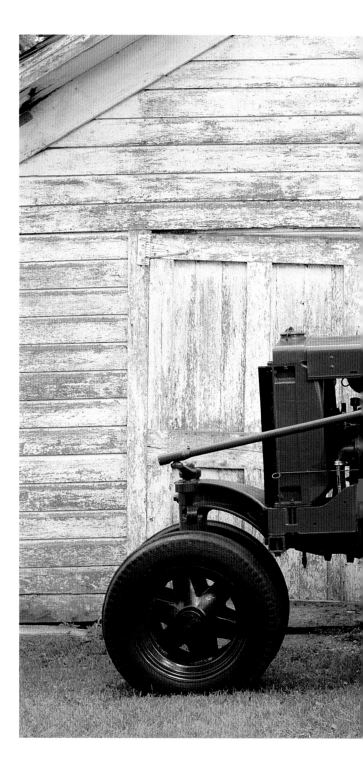

CHAPTER TWO

1930 - 1953

As early as 1922, farming researchers had concluded that the typical tractor was useful in 77 percent of field operations connected with the raising and cultivation of normal grain and 38 percent of row crops. It was the need for a tractor to be able to do a greater proportion of farming jobs that had led International to develop its Farmall, even though J. I. Case Plow Works had already shown what could be done with its 1919 Motor Cultivator—in reality a 12hp tricycle row-crop tractor. The Case Threshing Machine Co.'s crossmotor models were soon offered with special equipment to make them suitable for a wider range of work, including such specialties as rice and orchard work.

Joining the general-purpose L Model in 1929 was a smaller C Model, a 17–27hp machine intended not only for farming but also for more specialized service. Its most common variants were the CC row-crop tractor and the low-built and streamlined CO for use in orchards. The C models had four-cylinder overhead-valve engines developing up to 30hp at 1100rpm, three forward-speed gearboxes, and rear wheels that were adjustable for track from 48 to 84in.

The C was demonstrated to British farmers in March 1931 at Caynton Manor

Case Model RC, built in 1936 when the J. I. Case Company produced 3,500 R type tractors that year.

Nineteen thirty-six Case Model RC with Russel Church of Hil-Ray Farms, Minnesota City, Minnesota, at the controls. The four-cylinder 17 belt hp and 11 drawbar hp tractor was rated as a one- to two-bottom plow tractor.

Case Model RC with Albert Remme in the driver's seat. Albert's father bought the RC new in April 1936 when Albert was nine years old. The price was $630 at the local Case dealer, but he only had to pay $100, as he traded in a Fordson for $100, a team of young horses for $400, and an old drill for $30.

31

The Case L standard of 1938 has the four-cylinder engine rated at 30 belt hp and 26 drawbar hp. A three-speed transmission was standard, but

Case offered a high axle ratio for field and road use. 12mph could be accomplished in top gear.

and New Inn Farms, adjoining the famed Harper-Adams Agricultural College in Shropshire. Pulling a Ransomes three-bottom plow, it made light work of stiff land, thus equaling or even exceeding Case's claim that it was a "two- to three-plow tractor."

LEFT
Nineteen thirty-eight Case RC with the "chicken roost" steering. The best year for R sales with 6,200 produced. The RC had a Waukesha L-head, four-cylinder 17 belt hp engine with a three-speed transmission.

In 1935, CC models received an important addition: the Motor Lift, a forerunner of the hydraulic implement link. It was mechanically driven and consisted of a worm and wheel attached to the power take-off (PTO) that worked a lifting cam through a conventional clutch. Levers then relayed the motion to the rear drawbar and also, when required, to a front-mounted tool frame.

In addition to these developments, Case continued its pioneering work with grain harvesting. We have already noted its continuous involvement with threshing

Case Model R Industrial with Ed Schuth at the controls of his very rare tractor. Built in 1938, this R has electric start on the Waukesha 17 belt hp and 11 drawbar hp four-cylinder, L-head engine.

machines and their gradual replacement by combine harvesters from the 1920s. As early as 1905, Case was also involved in the automatic baler business and in 1932 surpassed most of its rivals with a one-man-operated combine driven from the PTO of a tractor. Versions with a separate Case power pack were also built for tractors without PTOs.

A contemporary brochure showed that the entire cost of fuel, let alone extra time, was less than the price of binder twine used under the old system of cutting and tying shocks. An ingenious feature was that the cutting header was hinged to the thresher so that undulating ground could be harvested more efficiently.

The latest Case balers were not the static variety that worked with threshing machines but tractor-drawn machines driven by PTO or donkey engine. These saved seventy-five cents to two dollars per ton compared with the old method. A farmer in Ithaca found he could bale twenty tons of heavy alfalfa clover and timothy-mixed hay in one afternoon. All users agreed that the ability to pick up hay just when the windrows were at their best was a great advantage with the new balers and tractors (now beginning to appear with pneumatic tires in place of iron wheels). Getting grain out of the field quickly so that it could be baled and the field replowed revolutionized farming.

The lean Depression years motivated farmers to increase their productivity by making their acreages viable. Those operators of family-owned farms that did use tractors had tended to buy the cheapest machines. To open up this market, in 1935 Case introduced a smaller two-plow RC with the usual three-speed transmission and roller chain transmissions of its sisters and using the proprietary Waukesha 11-17hp engine made by the Waukesha Motor Company of Waukesha, Wisconsin, to save development expenses. Not that Waukeshas were particularly cheap—indeed, they were reckoned to be some 20 percent more expensive than most rivals but in many respects better. This fitted Case's philosophy of using quality components. The RC models, available in a variety of forms, including a standard, general-purpose R, did a good job of bringing Case benefits to a wider market—even though fewer than 20,000 were sold and accounted for less than a quarter of Case's output of C and L models.

So now Case had a full range and lots of satisfied customers. Here is what a few of them had to say: According to J. W. Jobe of Torrington, Wyoming, what his tractor accomplished would be impossible using horses. Elex Theobald of Elkhart, Illinois, spent only eleven cents in repairs on his C over five years, not counting plugs and grinding-in the valves twice. Gunwald Nesbo of Shelby, Montana, found that after years of service, his speedy L still managed to save his crops from storm damage. When Russell Cahoone of Strong City, Kansas, overhauled his 1929 CC, he could find no

Case Model RI. The four-cylinder Waukesha engine has a 3-1/4x4in bore and stroke. Despite being a long stroke engine, the 17hp belt power is produced at a rather high 1425rpm.

wear in any bearing. Theo Paulson of Sedro Wooley, Washington, had run tractors and threshers for thirty-two years but found nothing to match his Case combination. Indeed, his C had run for 8–24hr per day for 230 days per year spread over five years, requiring only a fan belt, a set of piston rings, and an annual plug change. Another satisfied customer was R. D. Lynch of Manville, Alta, who commended the low fuel consumption of his L model. In nearly 10,000hr of use, its maintenance costs had averaged one cent per hour (including a set of replacement cylinders and pistons). After running three different makes of tractor on his 320-acre farm in Parker, South Dakota, Linden Flyger switched to a CC and after satisfaction with its predecessors had to concede that the Case did an altogether better job. Meanwhile, Marion Bergren used a similar tractor to do all the field work on 160 acres at Red Oak, Iowa, and especially liked the individual rear wheel brakes "to make square corners when plowing."

Edward Benreuter of Nashville, Illinois, found that he could do 90 percent of his work in the top gear of his Model C, and Byrd Clark of Goldendale, Washington, commended his L after eight years of use. He claimed that it was on its original magneto points yet still started easily. The three wide babbit-metal main bearings on the crankshaft gave virtually no trouble on any of these models. Most ran on low-grade fuel oil, and many owners commented on the extra traction provided by chain drive. Incidentally, the only wear that seems to have been recorded in the transmission was to the taper roller bearings, which could easily be taken up from the outside by removing shims by the Motor-Lift. The few who had invested in the Motor Lift praised the time it saved. Leo Murray of Dublin, Ontario, called his C "a snappy tractor on the belt."

Joe Gifford bought an RC instead of another team of horses for the lower price of $500 and found that his bank balance soon improved dramatically. This justified Case's claim that the day of the horse team was numbered, though the firm made less of the fact that the little RC could also plow more land in a day than his admittedly very elderly 12-25.

And finally, there is Herman Kruse of Franklin, Nebraska, who ran his Case for six trouble-free years, successfully replacing ten horses and two hired men with it.

The slogan used to sell the little RC was "Replaces the Last Team." This was a universal machine with rear track adjustable from 44 to 80in and a 543rpm PTO as standard equipment. Like the other models, it had removable cylinder sleeves and an oil wash air cleaner to protect them. The tricycle steering had variable geometry so that it was relatively direct when going straight ahead but progressively more highly geared on tight maneuvers. Case called this "synchronized"

Case RC built in 1938. The L-head, four-cylinder Waukesha engine is a high revving motor, yet it is smooth and quiet. However, the engine and governor did acquire a reputation for unreliability. The Zenith carburetor produced good gasoline consumption.

Case Model RC showing the Waukesha four-cylinder 17 belt hp engine and the PTO that was standard on this tractor. The fenders and Motor-Lift which lifted farm equipment via the transmission power take-off were extra. The RC was offered with single, dual cast front or extendible wide front track in iron or rubber tires.

LEFT
Case Model RC built in 1938. The RC proved very popular with farmers who had under 100 acres. Owned and beautifully restored by Norm Seveik of Northfield, Minnesota.

The standard-tread Case Model R of 1939. The first year of the Flambeau Red color. The Case dealer sign in the background is from the same period.

steering, which was aided by individual rear wheel foot brakes.

Among a wide range of matched implements was a finger bar mower mounted at the rear so that it could swing into line with the tractor if an obstacle was hit.

Case quietly acquired another implement maker in 1937, the Rock Island Plow Co. of Rock Island, Illinois. Established in the 1800s, this firm had entered the tractor business in 1914, initially by marketing the Heider. Rock Island soon took over production and made Waukesha- and Le Roi-powered models and, later, Buda and Waukesha engine types until 1936-1937.

Nineteen thirty-nine was an important year in the history of Case. Its whole range was restyled and changed in color, from grey to a more aggressive Flambeau Red. Flambeau means torch or fire-brand in French and implies a guiding light visionary—which is just what Case had been in its own quiet way. No doubt, this was what Case had in mind when picking the new look and shade, though changes under the skin were more in the line of gradual improvement rather than revolutionary. Best known of the new models was the replacement for the C, the three-plow DC, one of which the author's mother drove as a Land Girl in Britain during World War II.

The R fell into line both in color and less angular styling, and a whole range of other models followed. These had four-speed

The Model R Case was a well equipped tractor having standard PTO, differential brakes, fenders, and the Case roller-chain final drive, which did not sap the engine power as much as other designs.

Case Model R standard tread showing the cast-iron grill and Flambeau Red color which appeared in 1939. The major mechanical improvement over the 1938 model was the change from a three-speed to a four-speed transmission.

Albert Remme at the controls of his beautifully restored Model R Case. The compact 3,350lb tractor is powered by the four-cylinder Waukesha engine which is rated at 17 belt hp and 11 drawbar hp.

The Model R's Waukesha engine had a bad reputation for being weak. It is a high revver—1425rpm at normal engine speed. With faulty governors, it could easily be revved more. In the Nebraska tests of 1938, it produced much more power than it's classification of 20.52 belt hp and 15.58hp at the drawbar.

gearboxes and were to carry Case through to the 1950s. The S of 1940 effectively replaced the R and had a short stroke engine to permit higher revolutions. The original unitary construction Case, the L, became the four- to five-plow LA in 1940. These models had found an unusual niche in Britain as a waterproof tractor for launching lifeboats. The transformation was handled by Roadless Traction of Hounslow, a company that had originally made half-track versions of four-wheel-drive trucks to handle the task. It was later to achieve success as a converter of Fordsons to 4x4.

The V Series of Case tractors also began life in 1940, initially with a 15-22hp engine made by Continental, as also used by Massey-Harris. After a couple of years, Case readied its own four-cylinder unit for this model, which in its various versions eventually accounted for almost 150,000 sales. It used an all-gear transmission in place of a chain final drive and to save money, Case bought the gears ready-made. During the Flambeau Red period, Case consolidated its

The famous Case sunburst cast-iron Flambeau Red grill was introduced in 1939 on the model R and RC.

position as America's third-largest producer of tractors, selling half a million models.

During the war years, Case also introduced a new front-cutter 6ft combine and made wings for B-26 bombers, after-coolers for Rolls-Royce aircraft engines, anti-aircraft gun carriages, 500lb bombs, and hundreds of thousands of 155mm shells. At its peak, the company employed 8,400 people, and the return of peace brought new factories to Stockton, California; Bettendorf, Iowa; and Anniston, Alabama. The Anniston plant was subsequently re-sold in 1956.

The regime of new Case President Theodore Johnson in 1949 introduced a hydraulic three-point linkage named the Eagle Hitch in honor of the famous emblem of the company. It was first seen on the VA but soon replaced Motor-Lifts on the other models. Another novelty at the time was semi-diesel Hesselman engines in a few of the larger tractors. Waukesha had long been an enthusiastic exponent of the Swedish Hesselman system, but Case foresaw a greater future for the true diesel, which duly arrived in 1953.

Case Model R showing the tool box mounted on the differential housing. Inside this housing is the Case roller-chain final drive. Note the tractor number—4229737. To work out the year of production, combine the first numbers to make 42, then subtract the first number (4) away, which makes 38. That makes 1938 the build year. However, it is a totally original 1939 model painted Flambeau Red from new!

Tom Graverson, the Case collector from Bremen, Indiana, with his Airport Experimental Special, which he built in 1992. Note the air-cooled, four-cylinder Case combine engine, Case DC hood and fenders, and Bolens front wheels.

The Case RO Special, with owner and builder Loren Simmons from White, South Dakota. The R-type cast-iron sunburst radiator sur- round of 1939–40 hides the air-cooled A-125 Case combine engine.

PREVIOUS PAGES
The Case Model VC of 1941 proved a popular model with 8,160 built that year. The V Series was produced from 1940–1942 and the VA Series from 1942–1955. This model is owned and restored by Ed Lammers of Butterfield, Minnesota.

RIGHT
Case Model VC of 1941 with Continental L-head, four-cylinder engine rated at 22.07 belt hp and 15.07 drawbar hp. An impressive drawbar pull at the Nebraska tests on "irons" of 2,798lb.

Case Model VC of 1941. It was rated as a one- to two-bottom 12in plow tractor. J. I. Case Company bought the major components from other manufacturers. The 22 belt hp engine was built by Continental Motors, and the transmission and gears were produced by the Clark Company.

Case Model V standard of 1941. The V was the replacement for the Model R and was rated as a one- to two-bottom plow tractor. The standard production V was not as big a success as the VC. The VC sold 12,462, and the V standard only 2,321. This tractor is owned and restored by Norm Seveik.

Case Model V built in 1941. The Continental four-cylinder engine was rated at 22.07bhp on this 4,300lb tractor. The four speed trans- mission was built by the Clark Company. Owned and restored by Norm Seveik of Northfield, Minnesota.

1948 Case Model VAH. High-clearance row crop tractor with adjustable front and rear tread. Norm Seveik at the controls of his beautifully restored and rare VAH.

LEFT

Case Model VAH of 1948. The Case-designed engine was initially built by Continental Motors, but in 1947 Case produced the engine in-house at their Rock Island plant. This engine has a bore and stroke of 3-1/4x3-3/4in and produces 19 belt hp and 15 drawbar hp on gasoline. Owned by Norm Seveik.

1948 VAH. The high-clearance general-purpose tractor has a crop clearance of 27in. This model is the most collectable and interesting of the VAs. Nearly 150,000 VA tractors were manufactured, but only 2,016 were VAH high crops.

Case Model VAH GP high-clearance tractor of 1948. The four-cylinder 19 belt hp engine is mated to a four forward speed transmission giving a top speed of 12mph. Owned by Norm Seveik.

RIGHT
Case Model VAH of 1948. The VA Series was produced from 1942 through 1955, but the VAH was only available from 1947. The VA used an all-gear final drive and not the sprocket and roller-chain final drive of previous Case models. Owned and restored by Norm Seveik.

58

Case LA standard of 1949 with gasoline four-cylinder engine. The engine has a 4-5/8x6in bore and stroke and produces 52-1/2 bhp. Owned by Albert Remme.

LEFT
Case Model LA standard built in 1949 was rated as a four- to five-bottom plow tractor. The four-cylinder, overhead-valve engine produced 52.58 belt hp and 41.63 drawbar hp when tested in Nebraska.

Case Model LA standard of 1951 was rated as a four- to five-bottom plow tractor. The heavy duty LA tractor weighed 7,621lb with it's large and powerful 403ci four-cylinder Case engine producing 52.5 belt hp at a normal engine speed of 1100rpm. Owned by Russell Church.

LEFT
Case Model LA of 1951 showing the roomy platform and large seat that can be swung up or sideways. Notice the optional PTO on the differential housing.

Russell Church of Hil-Ray Farms in Minnesota City, Minnesota, giving his Model LA standard a high pressure wash. Although it was fitted with the optional electric start, Case still provided a hand crank.

LEFT
Nineteen fifty-one Case Model LA with it's styled radiator grill standing 61in high surrounding the massive radiator. The cooling system capacity is 15-1/4 gallons. The L and LA were the largest Case tractors produced in the 24-year period from 1929 through 1952. In 1946, no LAs were built due to the big strike at the Case factory.

The LA of 1951 was one of the last of the heavy-duty gasoline Case tractors. The large and heavy fuel consumption of the 58bhp Case engine necessitated the 30-3/4gal fuel tank. Case did offer low cost fuel LPG and Hesselman semi-diesel engines for better economy.

RIGHT
The Model SC built in 1951 was rated as a two 14in bottom plow tractor. The Case short-stroke, high revving, overhead-valve four-cylinder produced 21.6 belt hp at 1550rpm. This was a very popular tractor and is still being used by many farmers today. The adjustable rear tread, belt pulley, PTO, disc type brakes, hydraulic controls, and Eagle Hitch helped sales reach nearly 59,000 units.

CHAPTER THREE

1953 - 1975

Many of the models were carried through the mid-1950s, but a revised color scheme was introduced to correspond with the new 500 Series of 1953: Desert Sand for the sheet metal pressings and Flambeau Red for most of the rest. The 500 was effectively an uprated and improved LA but now with gas, LPG, or six-cylinder diesel options. The tractors came with full-electronics and double-disc brakes, and the diesel developed 32-56 drawbar horsepower on the Nebraska Test. This Test had become the standard of the industry ever since the state of Nebraska had brought in its own set of examinations to squelch the sale of inferior products, as had happened in the early days. In 1922, Nebraska ranked thirteenth in tractor concentration behind Wisconsin, California, Illinois, Ohio, Texas, Indiana, Iowa, Kansas, Minnesota, New York, Pennsylvania, and Missouri. A farmer-turned-politician in Nebraska had been sold a useless tractor in 1916, and he managed to persuade the state legislature to have all tractors examined by the Nebraska State University Department

This 1953 Case Model D is fitted with a Case mower and is still used on the farm by Albert Remme of Dennison, Minnesota. The D Series engine was similar to the Model C, with a 3-7/8x5-1/2in bore and stroke, but produced five more belt hp at 32.

Case Model D of 1953, the last year of production and the first tractor with a foot-operated clutch as standard equipment. The 7,000lb tractor with four-speed transmission was rated at 25 drawbar hp.

of Agriculture—where its famous Drawbar Test was devised. Manufacturers also had to establish service and spares facilities in relation to the number of tractors they sold. Overnight, the city slicker tractor salesman was obsolete.

So were some of Case's longest-running models from the 1930s–1940s, which were gradually ousted by the mid-range 400 and giant 600 in 1955 and finally by the little 300 in 1956. These were all high-grade and relatively expensive machines that did not sell in the numbers that they deserved. Consequently, Case moved to diversify

more heavily into the building construction and earth-moving field. Even though it had not actively marketed crawlers before, several of its tractors had been converted by outside specialists in the past. It had offered industrial and road-building tractors since the 1920s and had supplied various front-end loaders and dozers.

As a step to diversification, in 1957 Case acquired the American Tractor Corp. of Churubusco, Indiana. This firm had been making its Caterpillar- and Cletrac-rivaling Terratrac crawlers since 1950 and was early to offer both diesel engines and hydraulic lifts.

Case Model 500 diesel of 1953. The tractor LA owners had been waiting for. At last a fuel efficient powerful diesel engine with 10 percent more power than the LA. It now produced 64 belt hp.

Meanwhile, Case was developing a line of wheeled tractors, and in the same year that it acquired Terratrac introduced a new semi-automatic transmission known as Case-o-matic. Diesel engines under the name Dynaclonic were gradually standardized, the largest going in the Model 930 of 1962, billed a "King of the 6-plow Tractors." In the following year came the giant 1200 Traction King with a 451ci turbo diesel engine and four-wheel-drive. This engine was to last well into the 1970s and would be joined by a larger version of 504 "cubes."

The Model 500 of 1953 was the first Case agricultural diesel and the first six-cylinder engine manufactured by the Case tractor factory. This example is owned by Ed Lammers.

A 1954 Case Model 500 diesel. Evelyn Remme at work on their farm at Dennison, Minnesota. With husband Albert, they work the farm solely with Case tractors. The 500, even today, is still user-friendly with an efficient diesel engine, power steering, PTO, and rubber torsion-sprung seat.

At the other end of the scale, Case acquired the Colt Manufacturing Co., Inc., of Winneconne, Wisconsin, in 1964, which gave it access to 10 and 12hp garden tractors. From these grew a large range of similar Case machines for garden, utility, and industrial purposes. In the early 1970s, these included 8-16hp machines in the usual house colors, plus 14 and 16hp industrial loaders and backhoes with hydrostatic drive and, beginning in 1975, featuring the Power Yellow livery. At roughly the same

A Case 500 diesel built in 1954 with a six-cylinder 377ci engine producing 64hp at 1350rpm.

The 8,128lb tractor has power steering and a four forward speed transmission.

time, the construction equipment range was boosted by the acquisition of Macarr concrete pumps and placers, which henceforth were built at Case's Stockton plant. A new 450 crawler was joined by an 1150 that replaced the established 1000. Wheeled

four-wheel-drive loaders under the Case name had been assembled at the AWD-Michigan facility in Camberley, England, in the 1950s, prompting Case at the end of the decade to establish J. I. Case Company Ltd. in Britain to help revive the name in one of

A Case Model DC built in 1953 with the LPG. This model is also fitted with an adjustable front axle and Case loader. LP gas was available as standard equipment or for conversions from 1951.

its former best export markets. Australian, Brazilian, and French subsidiaries were also founded. The French business was based on the Vierzon premises where single-cylinder SFV tractors resembling Lanz or Marshall had until recently been produced. Allis-Chalmers also saw France as a likely springboard into Europe when it bought the Vendeuvre tractor business.

Case moved Terratrac production to its Burlington factory in 1961, consolidated wheeled tractor production at Rock

A Case Model DC built in 1953 with the LP gas option costing an extra $180. The four-cylinder, overhead-valve Case LP engine produced over 31 belt hp at 1100rpm, virtually the same as the gasoline engine.

Island with the greatly enlarged Clausen Works at Racine, and opened a vast new transmissions plant nearby to supply both the Tractor and Construction Equipment Divisions. In the mid-1960s, the company purchased a new site at Terre Haute, Indiana, which would become home to four-wheel-drive pivoting steer loaders and logging tractors and equipment. For the first time in the history of the industry, Case began offering its construction machinery for rental.

All these developments helped to disguise the fact that not all was well at Case. Like other old-fashioned engineering companies, Case had difficulty adapting to the winds of change. Diversification had helped to make it one of the Big Three in the construction equipment world, and its balers and harvesting machines were still leaders, though the tractors faced enormous competition.

Additional finance was needed to put Case on a sure footing. Help arrived in 1967,

Case 600 diesel built in 1957 with the six-cylinder 377ci engine producing 70hp at 1500rpm. The model had roller-chain final drive, hand clutch, and new–for–1957 six-speed transmission. Owner Ed Lammers is at the controls.

The 1958 Case 800 Series Case-o-matic with farmer and Case collector Ed Schuth in the operator's seat. The Case transmission can be selected from the direct gear ratios or the torque converter's range. This gave eight forward speeds in direct drive and eight in torque converter drive.

The Case Model 900 radiator and surround with the portable weights attached below. The 900 Series was offered in diesel (giving 70.24hp) and LPG (producing 71.05hp) using the same 377ci engine.

The Case Model 630 orchard diesel tractor built in 1962. J. R. Gyger, farmer and Case collector from Lebanon, Indiana, is at the controls.

LEFT
The Case Model 910B built in 1959 is an LPG model. The 377ci six-cylinder Case engine produces 71.05 PTO hp at 1350rpm. The transmission has six forward speeds, giving a top speed of 13.9mph.

when the company's largest shareholder since 1964, the Kern County Land Company of San Francisco, California, sold out to Tenneco Inc., of Houston, Texas. Tenneco was the world's largest distributor of natural gas and was also involved in oil,

chemicals, and packaging. Coincidentally, the new transmissions plant was just beginning series production. Case had a dramatic growing spurt.

Tenneco Chairman Nelson Freeman became Case Chairman and instigated massive reorganization and streamlining. One of the first victims was Old Abe, the bald eagle emblem, who was replaced in 1969 by an up-to-the-minute logo featuring the word "Case" on what looked like a tire or track print.

A new range of compact tractors and the firm's largest-yet combine harvester arrived in 1968. The following year saw the Agri-King line of tractors, of which the biggest was the four-wheel-drive Model 1470. All had fully enclosed cabs and Case's own engines, which in 1970 were rationalized to include 67- to 180-PTO horsepower open-chamber diesels with a high proportion of parts common to both four- and six-cylinder versions. A new line of little skid-steer loaders had been acquired from Uni-Loader, which proved popular for cleaning up farmyards. An altogether more-extensive range of diggers, cranes, excavators, and straddle carriers had arrived in the Case camp in 1968, when Tenneco bought Drott Manufacturing of Wausau, Wisconsin, a firm that had formerly been associated with International Harvester. Another acquisition was Davis Manufacturing of Wichita, Kansas, best known for its trenchers and tilt-bed trailers. By the time that the makers of Vibromax compactors in Germany joined the expanding business in 1970, Case had been fully absorbed by Tenneco, and

The Case Model 630-C diesel. The Case four-cylinder 188.4ci engine produced 48.85hp at a high 2250rpm.

several new products from log skidders to hydraulic excavators were in production or under development. Having bought CALSA, Spain's largest maker of wheeled loaders, Tenneco in 1972 was able to announce that Case had enjoyed its best year ever, with sales of $610 million.

The big news of 1972 was the purchase of David Brown Tractors by Tenneco. David Brown had existed as a gear maker since the nineteenth century and, like Case, had toyed with cars in the early years (and in the 1940s–1970s with Aston Martin and Lagonda). It had been a much later arrival on the implement and farm tractor scene, closely involved with the first production Fergusons in the 1930s. When Harry Ferguson transferred his allegiance to Ford (and then Standard, followed by Massey-Harris), David Brown entered the tractor business under its own name in 1939. Not surprisingly, in view of the Ferguson connection, Brown tractors had sophisticated hydraulics and achieved considerable success as the Cropmaster and the 900 Series of 1956. David Brown was also an important maker of implements following its absorption of Harrison McGregor & Co. Ltd. of Leigh, Lancashire, makers of Albion implements.

Henceforth, David Brown was to build many of the smaller tractors in Case's U. S. range and, in the same year that David Brown joined the fold, Case launched its 1175, 1270, 1370, and 2470 Agri Kings. At the bottom of the power range came the new 108, 118, 210, 224, 664, and 646 compact garden tractors.

The 2470 developed 176hp at the PTO and had an even more-powerful sister, the 2670, which could develop 221 PTO horsepower or 256bhp gross. Both used a turbo-charged 504ci diesel, which had the unusual feature of three separate cylinder heads to avoid distortion. These giant tractors were the third generation of modern Case 4x4s and unlike many of their rivals featured steering on both axles. To achieve this, Case used king-pin steering instead of hinged-chassis center-steering on so-called articulated tractors. Among the great advantages of the Case system was increased maneuverability. By steering just the rear wheels, the driver could hook up to implements more easily while front steering alone was appropriate for road use or minimal damage in row crop work with rear-mounted equipment. For a minimum turning circle, the front and rear wheels could be steered in opposite directions, whereas in certain circumstances crab-tracking could be useful. Examples included working on hillsides to counteract implement side-drift and to provide two lines of undisturbed land for the wheels to grip in wet conditions.

Putting the power down to the wheels was the job of three gears with on-the-go powershift between four ranges. Thus, twelve gears were provided to keep the machines operating at maximum output. The cab had heating and air-conditioning as standard equipment and was rubber

The Case Model 630 orchard tractor with the 188.4ci diesel engine. The 4,700lb tractor has twelve forward gears giving a top speed of 20.2 mph. Owned by J. R. Gyger.

mounted. It contained one of the most comfortable seats in the business, with adjustments for height, back, lumbar, armrests, and swivel.

The two-wheel-drive sisters of these big machines could have the same engine at lower turbo-charger boost or 401 or 451ci engines down to 93-PTO horsepower in naturally aspirated form. These had the twelve-speed power shift with seven gears in the critical 2–7mph range. Case claimed that these large, relatively unstressed seven main bearing engines gave longer life and more reserves of power. Daily plowing of up to forty acres was feasible with the broadly similar 1270/1370/1570 models. This was with six or seven bottom plows while disking with a twenty-eight-footer allowed up to 140 acres to be covered per day. Case made matching implements for all these tractors. Between them and the compacts came the David Brown range of 4x4 and 4x2 885/990/995/1210/1410 machines of 43- to 80-PTO horsepower. The 1410 4x4 had a two-speed PTO and oil-immersed disk "fiddle brakes." All included David Brown's familiar Selectamatic single lever depth, height, and traction controls.

In addition to these tractor and implement developments, the construction machinery side was booming, and in 1974 company sales as a whole exceeded one billion dollars for the first time.

A Case 870 Agri-King tractor collecting cattle feed from a Case W11B loader. The 870 was the first two-wheel-drive Case tractor to have hydrostatic power steering.

At this time, a new corporate color of Power Red and Power White was adopted on the agricultural tractors, and the David Brown name slowly disappeared from tractors and was phased out altogether in 1983. The garden tractor became Power Red with black and white accents.

The Case 870 Agri-King was manufactured between 1969 and 1973. It is powered by the 336ci four-cylinder Case engine rated at 70hp at 1900rpm. It is seen here at the Hil-Ray Dairy Farm of Minnesota City, Minnesota, with Jared driving.

Case 70 Series Agri-King 1070 two-wheel-drive tractor. The Case cab is rubber-mounted for isolation of noise and vibration.

Case Agri-King 1070 with six-cylinder 451ci diesel engine producing 108hp at 2100rpm.

There was no option of gasoline or LPG engines. The 11,410lb tractor has eight forward gears.

CHAPTER FOUR

1975 ONWARDS

Because making large engines in relatively small numbers was not a paying proposition, Case in the mid-1970s decided to buy proprietary engines, as it had done occasionally in the past. It chose Scania engines for its giant 300bhp 2870 Traction King 4x4 machine and placed an order for 1,100 DS11 turbo-charged units, designed in Sweden but built at Sao Paulo in Brazil. The same engine was also supplied to Case's new Brazilian front-loader plant at Sorocaba.

Another international link in the mid-1970s came when Case decided to market the Unimog general-purpose and agricultural load carrier and tractive unit in North America. The 346ci 94bhp version with eight- or twenty-speed transmission, an optional PTO, and three-point linkage was chosen. "Case—the Tractor Specialist," as the company now prided itself, entered into the American bicentennial celebrations of 1976 with a Stars and Stripes livery on its "Spirit of '76" limited-edition version of the 1570.

This and its sisters came with a new customer service package that included the usual factory and dealer inspections but now had the added dimensions of a

The Case "Spirit of 76" is a two-wheel-drive Model 1570 tractor painted in bicentennial colors for 1976. The turbo-charged, six-cylinder 504ci diesel engine was rated in the Nebraska tests at 180.4 PTO hp at 2100rpm. The Spirit has a twelve forward speed transmission.

A Case Model 970 Agri-King set up for pumping silage. This model was built from 1969 to 1978 with the six-cylinder 401ci Case diesel engine. During the first two years of production, the diesel engine gave 85hp at 1900rpm; it was then upgraded to 93hp at 2000rpm. A gasoline engine of 377ci producing 85hp was offered. It was cheaper to buy but not to run.

full check after 100–200hr of service before six months had elapsed. Anything that required attention was then supplied free of charge, with the exception of lubricants and filters.

The cabs had been subtly improved and were tested to withstand roll-over and rear-up damage. An ingenious feature was an air filter that collected dust before it could enter the driver's air space. The dust was then expelled at the upper rear each time the door was shut.

The old SFV tractor plant in France started to build its 580F loader/backhoe in 1976 to complement others in the Case range, including the Drotts. During 1980, the ten-thousandth 580F was sold and a new site to build crawler loaders was selected at Redruth in Cornwall, United Kingdom, now production headquarters of the small skid-steer loaders. To strengthen Case's performance in this field, at a time when tractor sales were suffering across the industry, Case entered into a joint venture with the French hydraulic excavator and crane manufacturer Poclain. Case bought a 40 percent stake in Poclain in 1977 and acquired outright its facilities in Great Britain, West Germany, Spain, Belgium, and Brazil. Drott soon began building Poclain equipment in the United States.

In 1979, an order for 2,000 rough-terrain forklift trucks for the U. S. Army contributed to the company's first two billion-dollar sales year. By then, David Brown factories had been modernized at a cost of £15 million, and the new unified 90 Series of tractors had replaced the 70 Series. These included 4x2 and 4x4 machines with unique solid-state selective steering mechanisms.

In 1980, Case started a joint venture diesel engine factory with the Cummins Engine Co. The title chosen for this new business was Consolidated Diesel Company and manufacturing began near Rocky Mount, North Carolina. To commemorate

The Case 2670 Traction King articulated 4WD tractor built from 1974 to 1978. The 20,810lb tractor was the first Case tractor to have a turbo-charger and an intercooler.

Case 2670 Traction King with 504ci six-cylinder, turbo-charged and intercooled diesel engine producing 219 PTO hp at 2200rpm.

After over twenty years of daily use, a small black cloud appears from the exhaust at maximum revolutions.

Case's long and illustrious history, a statue of Jerome Increase Case was erected at Racine, the original office building was given protected status by the Landmarks Preservation Commission, and a 1913 steam traction engine was restored for company use.

Tractor developments in the 1980s included the addition of micro-electronic controls on the 4x4 versions of the 90 Series from 1981. Mechanical front-wheel-drive options for the 2090 and 2290 came in 1982,

when a special 4690 was developed for Canadian conditions. In 1983 came the 94 Series, initially only with 4x2 in the 43–180bhp band but soon afterwards with 4x4. The 4494 to 4994 range of 1984 covered 210- to 400-gross bhp, the largest being powered by V8 turbo diesels. From the smallest model upwards, there was the availability of four-wheel-drive while those with Hydra Shift had the benefit of full engine braking, an unusual feature with semi-automatic trans-

The Case 2670 Traction King tractor. The wheel treads are adjustable all around and can run four, eight, or twelve tires, depending on terrain. The colors are Case Power Red and Power White which were introduced in 1974.

mission. A well-insulated cab kept interior noise below 85dB, and there were improved hydraulics with assisted rams. All these tractors had a new Power Red with black and white accents color scheme, and the construction equipment dubbed a new look in Power Tan and brown.

Features of the 94 Series included an "Intelligence Center." This contained imperial and metric readouts, function monitoring system, counters for elapsed time and acreage, a wheel position indicator on the 4x4, multi-dry disc brakes, air/oil suspension seat, hydrostatic steering with adjustable column, and the usual twelve-speed power shift transmission on the Hydra-Shift semi-automatic transmission. The smaller models were made in the former David Brown facility at Meltham in Huddersfield, United Kingdom.

One of the most important events in the history of the North American and

A 1991 Case International 9280 built in the Steiger factory which became part of Case Tenneco in 1986. The four-wheel-drive articulated tractor is powered by the six-cylinder, turbo-charged, inter-cooled Cummins NTA-885 diesel engine. The 855ci power unit is rated at 375hp and gives maximum torque of 1,266lb-ft at 1400rpm.

European tractor and farm machinery industry took place at the end of 1984, when parts of the mighty International Harvester empire were acquired by Tenneco.

International Harvester had been formed in 1902 from a group of companies, many of which owed their origins to the pioneering work of Cyrus McCormick and William Deering. International tractors had become a major force in the industry with such early landmarks as the Mogul, Titan, Junior, 10-20, Farmall, and dozens of subsequent tractors. In the end, the company became almost too big and too diversified. The collapse of the tractor market that had adversely affected Case around 1980 (it had barely broken even in 1982) had disastrous consequences for the overstretched International Harvester Corp. The important truck manufacturing side was reformed under the name Navistar, and Tenneco/Case picked up the agricultural pieces.

This catapulted Case to second place in the industry in 1985 with a full line of tractors and equipment and a greatly expanded dealer network. The Case and International emblems were united in a color scheme of International Red with Case Black/silver stripe, and much of the International tractor range above 95hp was axed. This helped to reduce massive over-capacity in the industry and included machines that had been brought in from other manufacturers to round out the International range. In a desperate bid to offer tractors for every potential use, International had been buying its smallest 4x4 machines from Mitsubishi and its largest from Steiger. It had a vested interest in doing so, having owned approximately one-third of the Steiger business in Fargo, North Dakota, between 1975 and 1982. Climbing from small beginnings in the late 1950s, Steiger had become the largest producer of giant tractors in the United States, but this did little to help International Harvester, which had disposed of its shareholdings before the takeover. Later, in 1986, Tenneco reversed the process by acquiring Steiger outright. The Tenneco takeover added International's two manufacturing plants in North America and five in Europe. The European operations of Case International Harvester had sales exceeding

£750 million and employed 12,000, nearly half of them in Britain. International's plant at Doncaster was helping Meltham to produce nine models in the 45–108hp sector and, in 1986, benefited from a £30-million refurbishment as part of a £90-million U.K. package spread over five years. The Carr Hill plant at Doncaster, which had been closed for three years, was redeveloped to produce two formerly American tractor models, the 1896 and 2096, as well as transmission units for combines and cotton pickers. Meanwhile, the 3394 and 3594 models featured twelve- or twenty-four-speed power shift and mechanical front-wheel-drive. Implements were improved, and a new generation of Axial-Flow combine harvesters developed.

Poclain was gradually absorbed into the Case International Harvester core business, and overall manufacturing capacity was decreased in America and increased in Europe. Beginning in 1987, a "world tractor" range with Consolidated Diesel engines was built in Europe for worldwide distribution. By the 1990s, tractors were being produced in America at Racine and Fargo (giant 4x4), in Australia at St. Mary's, in England at Doncaster and Meltham, in France at St. Dizier (loaders carried on at Vierzon), and in Germany at Neuss. Implements were made at some of these and several other plants while East Moline specialized in combines.

The Case International Harvester range is now the market leader in many areas and one of the top three virtually everywhere. The range of tractors, as this brief survey of Case is concluded in 1994, consists of eight different series. These incorporate everything the David Brown, International Harvester, Steiger, Case, and all their associates have learned about tractor design in recent years. These include the low-profile 3200 Series for dairy and mixed farming in the 52–60hp range. The 2100 Series includes 55–75hp machines with twelve forward and twelve reverse synchromesh gears. The twenty forward and nine reverse-gear 1455 is intended for highly efficient PTO work while the Maxxum Plus is a highly versatile performer in the 90–125hp class. The Magnum 7000 Series, like many of its contemporaries, has 4x4 as standard, with king-pin steering on its smaller front wheels and an 8.3ltr diesel delivering 155–264bhp, depending on the level of turbo boost. The lower-output models have synchromesh and the largest 24+6 reverse power shift. At the top in terms of horsepower, weight, and drawbar pull comes the 14ltr 380bhp 9280. This weighs sixteen tons, has pivoting steer, and boasts a twelve-speed power shift transmission that allows skip-shifting to waft the machine via first, fourth, sixth, and eighth gears to 12kph in just 3sec. It is intended for much the same purpose on the prairies as the famous Case Gold Medal winner of 1911—but there the comparison ends.

Jerome Increase Case, not to mention Cyrus McCormick and William Deering, would be amazed by what has grown from those first small seeds they sowed more than 150 years ago.

INDEX